Table of Contents

The Angel Gabriel Appears to Me 1

The Angel Gabriel Reflects on the Nature of Belief 3

The Angel Gabriel Talks Me Off the Ledge 4

The Angel Gabriel Brought Me a Message 5

The Angel Gabriel Makes Me a List of the Heavens 6

The Angel Gabriel Texts Me Pictures from His First Week on Earth 8

The Angel Gabriel Says It's Not a Booty Call if He Doesn't Have Genitals, 10

The Angel Gabriel Goes Black Friday Shopping 11

The Angel Gabriel Throws a Baby Shower 12

The Angel Gabriel is on a Mission 13

TV Teaches The Angel Gabriel How to Be Human 14

The Angel Gabriel Texts Me Pictures From His Travels on Earth 15

The Angel Gabriel Goes to Open Mic Night 17

The Angel Gabriel Ditches the Nature Walk 18

The Angel Gabriel Cheats at Scrabble 19

The Angel Gabriel Tries to Ghost Me 23

The Angel Gabriel Texts Me at the End of the World 24

Interview With the Author 27

(Text) Messages from The Angel Gabriel

The Angel Gabriel Appears to Me

in a dream

upon waking

in the bathroom mirror, a warped form through the
      showerfog

in my mentions, liking every post

in a pop-up ad for rehab

on each street corner; sometimes a busker, saxophone
      to heavenly lips, sometimes waiting on the
      wingless man for permission to walk

at the gym, lifting too much weight for too many reps

at the deli, puzzling over the mystery of the jalapeño
      popper

in the checkout line, scanning my razor blades and
      formal wear

in the lounge, restocking the K-cups

at a Monster Truck rally, polishing the chrome hubcaps
      of the winning truck

at the beach, wrestling with an umbrella

in the highest branches of the cherry tree, raining
blossoms on the sidewalk around me

at the trailhead, obscuring the signs

at the museum

in every painting

at the party, falling out of the pinata

on all 52 cards in the deck

in traffic, blocking my attempt to merge

as a voice harmonizing with the AM band static

in the coin-only toll booth

on a Lion's Den billboard advertising earthly delights

at the scene of the accident, taking insurance
information

in my peripheral vision, no matter how quickly I turn
my head

The Angel Gabriel has appeared to me so often, in
places familiar and foreign; when he stands on my
doorstep, swinging bulb of the porchlight casting a
flickering halo, I think nothing of letting him in

2

The Angel Gabriel Reflects on the Nature of Belief

I don't believe in angels, but The Angel Gabriel says belief is not a requirement. He is not Tinkerbell, languishing from lack of applause. He equally rejects humanity's sincere belief in guardianship, is bemused when I show him online purchasing portals for charms and bumper stickers and nursery decor which announce a protective presence. There are entire virtual forums dedicated to accounts of angelic intervention, but The Angel Gabriel's only response is that holy dictum: correlation does not equal causation.

I don't believe in angels, yet The Angel Gabriel makes himself comfortable. He takes off his shoes, uses the last of my creamer, opens the blinds to let the night attend us from its perch atop the skyline. When he inventories the contents of my apartment, he moves with the delicate caution of a being used to taking up space. On one shelf stands a collection of ceramic figurines. He runs his fingers through the air above them, barely not touching. Leopard, Rhino, Otter, Porpoise. A zoo sent them to me in exchange for some of the ones and zeroes in my bank account. Tiger, Tortoise, Saola, Penguin. I have never seen the animals they signify. Lion, Tuna, Panda, Wrasse.

I don't believe in angels, and The Angel Gabriel encircles me. He guides my hands to order the figurines into neat rows, into parallel lines that define and boundary, that prescribe and order and reject my unbelief.

The Angel Gabriel Talks Me Off the Ledge

On my therapist's orders, I am making a pros and cons list before I do something I might regret. The Angel Gabriel thinks he would have made a good therapist. He has a calming presence, and enjoys the shape of his mouth when he says the phrase, "how does that make you feel?" While I make my list, he stands at the mirror in one of my turtlenecks, trying on different listening faces. The pros list is the usual drudgery of a mind folding in on itself again and again like a piece of notebook paper passed from hand to schoolgirl hand. The cons list is everything The Angel Gabriel tells me they don't have in heaven: neon signs shaped like flamingos, and walls on which to hang paintings of dubious quality. Heaven has trains but no train-tracks, nothing to walk down while avoiding the future. Since Heaven has no soil it has no plants, just one endless desert. There is no wind in Heaven, and therefore no wind chimes clinking softly in the predawn. No cats, only guinea pigs. No insects either, which means no dragonflies skimming the water. No water.

When the list is finished, The Angel Gabriel says we should celebrate by going out for all the foods they don't have in Heaven. He looks sharp in my turtleneck as we share brussels sprouts, french fries, egg rolls. We pass a spoon back and forth, trading bites of black cherry ice cream.

4

The Angel Gabriel Brought Me a Message

but forgot it the second he saw his first cat video. He
knows the message was important but not why, does not
know whether it would have ended war or offered a balm
to the Twelve Infinite Sadnesses of the human condition.
The Angel Gabriel has taken seven showers and five long
walks hoping the message will come back to him, but it's
still there dancing on the tip of his tongue like his cousins
on the head of a pin, infinite and out of reach.

The Angel Gabriel Makes Me a List of the Heavens

Guitarist heaven is the flawless strum of the six-string F, each note a pebble dropped into a well.

Blender heaven is power surge, ecstatic blade-whirl.

Dog heaven is the rug, the hearth, the dream, the leg thumping in the dream, the sweet stroke of the hand on the head while the dream spools out like a dropped bobbin.

Rhyme heaven is the limerick.

God heaven is the cessation of prayer, silence falling across the whole universe of its imagining.

Parent heaven is the exhale after the child is safely asleep, but before they are missed.

Trash heaven is the hand of the man who pulls it from the heap, holds it to the light, calls it treasure.

Wave heaven is the crest.

Boat heaven is the trough.

White lady heaven is a Black woman reassuring her she's one of the good ones.

Son heaven is the disinheritance.

Gun heaven is the holster.

Coyote heaven is pursuit, the perpetual dust of the roadrunner hovering above the horizon.

Hi-fi heaven is the flawless needle drop, sound swell filling the empty room.

Gamer heaven is up-up-down-down- left-right-left-right-B-A-start.

Puppet heaven is the hand withdrawing.

Sushi heaven is the skillet.

Lice heaven is the playroom.

Light heaven is the prism.

Hypothesis heaven: the theory; theory heaven: the law; law heaven: the exception.

Teacher, spider, hacksaw, hotdog, pixel, chicken, drumset, rabbit; for each being on this plane its own heaven, uniquely designed, distinct in flavor and finish—

Angels? He says. There is no heaven for angels.

The Angel Gabriel Texts Me Pictures from His First Week on Earth

ooo
is this creation

[image description: churning waves under a
        cloudlocked sky]

ooo
is this pentecost

[image description: a wildfire evacuation order]

ooo
is this conversion

[image description: a rodeo clown being thrown by a
        horse]

ooo
is this communion

[image description: a sample tray covered in pigs in a
        blanket]

ooo
is this trinity

[image description: on a bend in the highway, a trio of
        crosses]

ooo
is this rapture

[image description: an empty pair of shoes dangling
          from a telephone line]

ooo
is this covenant

[image description: a "no soliciting" sign on the
          cathedral's locked doors]

The Angel Gabriel Says It's Not a Booty Call if He Doesn't Have Genitals,

and he doesn't. He comes over at three am, pulls down his joggers and shows me what he calls "the light of pure goodness." The light seems mediocre at best, but I go along with it. The Angel Gabriel wants intimacy in these smallest hours of the morning, so we compare embarrassing adolescent photos, me with my endless emo bangs, him with his infinite number of eyes. He lays on my bed, head hanging over the edge, legs stretched up against the wall. We kiss once, as sunrise checks its watch on the other side of the horizon, but The Angel Gabriel doesn't know how. He pulls his lips all the way back, meets mine with his perfectly straight, dry teeth. We lay side by side, and I fall asleep somewhere in the middle of The Angel Gabriel telling me which US Presidents are in hell, which is all of them. In the morning, the pillow still holds the indent of his head.

The Angel Gabriel Goes Black Friday Shopping

The rush and press of bodies reminds him of the throngs outside the gates of heaven, makes him nostalgic for the Sunset Gardens that rotate above the earth so that it's always dusk, always jasmine on the breeze, always bees returning to their apiaries to unload their treasures. The Angel Gabriel brings me back a floor lamp that is too tall for the tallest room in my apartment. No amount of angelic calculation or distortion can make it fit. At first we are silent on the drive back to the store, but soon he is telling me about the gates, how the only hell is the crowd, the waiting, the unobscured view of paradise through the vine-twined bars. He tells me how a feature of heaven is the white-noise murmur of the unlucky ones, *there but for the grace of God go we*. Our return is denied, all sales final. We leave the lamp on the sidewalk. In the rearview mirror I see it: the lamp peering through the store's front window, on the outside looking in.

The Angel Gabriel Throws a Baby Shower

Because it's tradition, the shower is held at night

Because it's tradition, cool June breezes tease the
   curtains

Because it's tradition, the cupcakes are unleavened,
   the punch unspiked

Because it's tradition, The Angel Gabriel arrives late

Because it's tradition, he brings nothing good

Because it's tradition, I am troubled in my heart

Because it's tradition, he invites only men who are not
   the father: his bus driver, his least favorite
   barista, his best friend's dog

Because it's tradition, I am silent while the party
   happens around me

Because it's tradition, I am untouched

The Angel Gabriel is on a Mission

to learn everything he can about life on Earth: an attempt at quality control. Working at a self-serve frozen yogurt shop in the richest country on the planet is probably not the best place to get a comprehensive understanding of the human experience, but The Angel Gabriel likes toppings. Chocolate chips, raspberries, sprinkles. One night after a shift, The Angel Gabriel tells me he spent an hour contemplating the mystery of the Nilla wafer.

College students come into the shop late at night for a cup of vanilla-berry and the aloof beauty of an angel under fluorescent lights, half-apron tied to emphasize his narrow waist.

I email The Angel Gabriel suggestions for further work experience: articles about millet farmers in Gambia, rohu fishermen in Myanmar, salteña vendors in Bolivia, jobs where workers earn less in a day than it would take to buy a child-sized cup of pina colada swirl. The Angel Gabriel marks them all spam.

When his mission is over, The Angel Gabriel tells me he will open a shop that sells only toppings. This will cut out the middle man, allow patrons to divest of the illusion that they are there for anything other than permission to eat Reese's pieces by the spoonful.

This, he says, is his chosen purpose: to reveal us to ourselves.

TV Teaches The Angel Gabriel How to Be Human

/Mork's rainbow suspenders / E.T.'s luminous finger / Johnny 5 lobbing insults at his mechanical brethren / Air Bud panting as the shot clock expires / The Brother from Another Planet laying healing hands on a wounded video game / Robin Williams carving the delicate wood of the clock / Milla's bandage-strap jumpsuit / Remy the Rat's recipe book / Stitch's spangled Elvis costume / WALL-E watching Hello Dolly! on repeat, one metallic hand holding the other / Thandiwe Newton watching prairie grass wave / Scarlett Johansson's voice choosing the infinite space between numbers / Starman Jeff Bridges resurrecting the deer / The Thing / The Host / The Fly / Clark Kent / Joe Black / Star-Lord / Frankenstein's Monster / Frankenstein's Monster's Bride / Barbie / Chucky / M3gan / The Cylons / The Prawns / The Coneheads / Chihiro's parents brushing the sty from their clothing / John Malkovich in his tuxedo walking down the center of the highway / The Terminator learning why we cry / Janet's reset button / Data's emotion chip / Marcel's shoes at the lip of the grave / Regan kissing the cheek of the priest as he leaves / The Iron Giant embracing an oncoming missile like a lover / Pinocchio perching on the edge of the pool table, wooden heart splintered with fear / Ariel's silence / Harry's despair as Lithgow turns his back / Hogarth alone / Eric leaving / Eve leaving / Dolores alone / George leaving / Connie leaving / Lilo alone / Theodore alone / John Connor alone / Linguine leaving / Josh leaving / Jenny alone / Frankie alone / Portia alone / Korben leaving / Stephanie leaving / Chris alone / Haku leaving / Jason leaving / Spock alone / New York alone / Gepetto alone / Mindy leaving / Elliot leaving /

The Angel Gabriel Texts Me Pictures From His Travels on Earth

ooo
this is baptism

[image description: a pasture gate stands open. In the background, alpacas lower their heads to the stream]

ooo
this is anointment

[image description: a palm oil factory on the outskirts of Freetown. In the foreground, laborers line up to wash work from their hands]

ooo
this is confirmation

[image description: two soldiers standing at the edge of the DMZ, looking north. One rests their hand on the other's shoulder]

ooo
this is eucharist

[image description: the banks of the Peace River poisoned by swaths of water hemlock]

ooo
this is matrimony

[image description: a collage of highway signs commissioned by unfaithful husbands: Adelaide, Maryborough, Alice Springs]

ooo
these are holy orders

[image description: a leopard seal ordaining the spray-tossed rocks of the Gould Coast. Between its flippers, remnants of penguin]

ooo
this is penance

[image description: a crack through the foundation of the British Museum]

The Angel Gabriel Goes to Open Mic Night

He tries a joke first about the difference between a crow and a raven, but the punchline relies on a level of avian knowledge the audience just doesn't have. The tables are filled with college students looking for the medication of a cheap drink, and skeptical tourists lured in by the marquee's promise of Comedy! and five dollar pitchers. When he sits down, slick with flop sweat where his Adam's apple should be, The Angel Gabriel says the moment between the punchline and the absence of laughter is the closest he has ever felt to being human. A host of empty glasses assembles on the table between us as he tells me that being God's messenger on Earth used to mean something. At last call, The Angel Gabriel goes back up on stage and reveals the true meaning of life, though most of the bar's patrons are too deep in their pitchers to hear.

The Angel Gabriel Ditches the Nature Walk

All things are less impressive when you were present at their creation. The Angel Gabriel ambles behind the group as it moves through the cedars, pointedly ignoring the guide. The talk at the trailhead was about stewardship, about how to admire the plants we encounter while leaving them living. The Angel Gabriel strips each shield fern of its fronds, leaving the naked stalks strewn among the trail rocks like splinters fallen from the broken gates of Eden. He plucks fireweed blooms to crush between thumb and forefinger. He pops baneberries into his mouth for the cyanotic satisfaction of surviving that which would kill any mortal being. Our guide comments that she has never seen so few animals on a hike, says they must all have business in other parts of the forest. The Angel Gabriel scoffs that only humans are foolish enough to approach angels. By the time we reach the lookout he has vanished, and it is not until I get back to the apartment that I find him wrapped in an afghan, Attenborough's honey rumble voice pouring over shots of steaming southern rainforests. It's not quite sibling rivalry, The Angel Gabriel tells me, this tension between his kind and creation. It's the feeling the harvested crop has as the farmer turns their back to look out over the fresh, untilled field.

The Angel Gabriel Cheats at Scrabble

He plays *quotidian*, *larynx*, and *xenophobe*. He plays
omnibus and *liminal*. He challenges *xerxes* for its proper
noun status even though he is winning by 212 points. He
swears he is not looking through my palette to perceive
my letters, but he has blocked my last three plays. The
man who taught The Angel Gabriel this game found
religion in prison. In his memory, The Angel Gabriel plays
lock and *dam*, plays *wall* and *time*. A standard Scrabble set
has 100 tiles, one for each of the Languages of Heaven.
We have amassed twice that number on the board before
I notice the chorus that escapes the felt bag every time it
is opened. When I say I won't play with cheaters, The
Angel Gabriel shows all he has learned from human men
by flipping the board. For weeks I find little reminders:
letter tiles under the couch cushions, behind the
bookshelf, on my tongue, the wood tasteless as sacred
host.

The Angel Gabriel Exits the Movie Montage

Song: "Angel" by Fleetwood Mac plays over montage

Int. Kitchen- Morning

Wide shot of the ceiling, where flour swarms and dives through the air like a flock of swallows, like the wheeling legions of the heavenly guard. Slow pan down to the table, where the flour-cloud dusts The Angel Gabriel's shoulders, ends up everywhere except the bowl set out for pancake batter.

The Angel Gabriel's partner stands at the edge of the frame, hands on hips, surveying the wreckage— abandoned dishes, flour-caked fixtures—before moving to begin the clean up.

Cut to:

Ext. City Park- Day

Tracking shot of The Angel Gabriel exploring a cobbled path. Moss coats each stone as he walks, leaving a trail of green footprints in his wake. He looks back over his shoulder, beckons to his partner, who hesitates for a moment before following.

Cut to:

Ext. Zoo- Day

The Angel Gabriel stands in front of the flamingo pond watching the birds bump chests, a repeating motif of hearts forming and breaking. He gestures to the birds, expecting a response. When he looks up, The Angel Gabriel sees that he is alone. His companion has moved on to another exhibit.

                                                    Cut to:

Ext. Apartment Building- Midnight

Pebbles spatter against the window, arrhythmic invitations. A high-angle shot shows The Angel Gabriel on the street, smiling at the camera. He holds up an offering, a bouquet of ornamental cabbages. A light comes on in the window, and his companion appears in silhouette. The window does not open. The light goes out.

                                                    Cut to:

Int. Restaurant- Evening

The waiter shows The Angel Gabriel to his regular table, set for two. The Angel Gabriel waits, expectantly, anxiously smoothing the borrowed turtleneck over his chest and shoulders. Time passes. Eventually he stands, looking down at the wilted brussel sprouts, the melted ice cream. After a long pause, he walks out of the shot.

Ext. Waterfront- Dawn

Fog shrouds the channel. There is no one in the frame.

Cut to:

Int. Airport Terminal- Day

An empty concourse. There is no one running through it, no one desperate to reach the plane in time.

Cut to:

Ext. City Park- Night

Summer rain falls on the roof of the gazebo, each drop a kiss. There is no one in the frame.

Cut to:

A series of shots in quick succession: Kitchen, Zoo, Waterfront, Park, Apartment. In each location there is no one in the frame. The song continues to play, but the sound fades.

End montage.

The Angel Gabriel Tries to Ghost Me

but he doesn't know how to leave without fire and flood. He walks around my apartment putting things out of place: toothpaste in the junk drawer, scissors under the sink, clean clothes balled between couch cushions. The Angel Gabriel stands around clearing his throat and asking for things he has hidden until I reassure him of how sad I would be if he left. Secure once again in his rightful position as the object of desire, The Angel Gabriel gives me a going away present: a faceted stone pulsing with unearthly light. He says if I swallow the stone it will lodge in my core, keeping me warm on long nights alone. Angels do not have terrestrial digestive systems. After The Angel Gabriel leaves, I put the stone in a tupperware, which I put in a cabinet. Despite this double enclosure, opal light leaks out around the hinges. The silent kitchen is illuminated, stage set for a visitation which has come and gone.

The Angel Gabriel Texts Me at the End of the World

ooo
this was devotion

[image description: a hairbrush on the lip of the
        bathroom sink, morning light limning each barb
        on the downy feather caught in the bristles]
ooo
this was liturgy

[audio file: a zipper being undone, a mattress taking
        the weight of a body]

ooo
this was ministry

[image description: a row of glasses neatly loaded into a
        dishwasher]

ooo
this was revelation

[audio file: a shower running; under the fall of water,
        snatches of a voice singing, "someone to watch
        over me."]

ooo
this was grace

[image description: a pizza, half intact, the other half
        dotted with negative space circles where the
        olives used to be]

ooo
this was providence

[audio file: the held breath between the opening of a
        question and the closing of the answer]

ooo
this was incarnation

[image description: a queen bed, one side is neatly made,
        blankets tucked and smoothed; the other side
        rumpled, sheets twisted, pillow dented]

Interview With the Author

Q&A with Tiffany Woodley

1. This collection is a fascinating exploration of the relationship between the human and the divine. How would you want a reader to summarize the arc of the relationship between the speaker and The Angel Gabriel?

When I started putting this collection together, I wanted it to map the stereotypical arc of a short-term relationship: from the couple meeting to learning more about each other and getting settled, to the eventual breakup. The major thing that makes this relationship arc different is that one half of the couple is a divine, immortal Archangel. Other than that, though, I wanted the relationship to feel both authentically engaging and authentically frustrating from the perspective of the speaker. I really hoped to evoke divinity more in the sense of Greek mythology, with a figure that is both divine and fallible.

2. Though we come to know The Angel Gabriel through his thoughts and actions, the speaker is less specific. What are the key aspects of that character?

My vision of the speaker was always as someone who is a lapsed believer, not practicing. I envision someone who grew up in the church and has a familiarity with religious lore due to their upbringing. This seemed an important quality that might allow The Angel Gabriel to insist himself into the speaker's life more easily. Another key aspect of the speaker's character is that this is someone who is very passive and has a deeply held belief that the things that happen to them in life are entirely outside of their control. They feel pretty powerless to influence any part of their relationship to others, and powerless to influence The Angel Gabriel in any of the choices he makes on Earth. It was important to me, in the revising process, to make sure that the speaker feels very gender neutral. I want readers of any gender to be able to find entry points into the narrative and to be able to relate to the speaker.

3. What drew you to this narrative in particular? What is it about The Angel Gabriel that you feel tied to over other angels?

The first piece of the manuscript I wrote was "The Angel Gabriel Talks Me Off the Ledge." I have to admit, at the time, I didn't think for a moment that I would write an entire collection around this character. When writing that first piece, I picked The Angel Gabriel because of his role as a messenger. When the collection was finished and it was time for revisions, I did question whether I should pick a different angel, but I chose to stick with The Angel Gabriel because he is the angel who appears most frequently in the Bible. In each biblical appearance, he brings a message to someone, most famously to the Virgin Mary. I thought that The Angel Gabriel would be the most recognizable to readers, especially since his role as a messenger has permeated popular culture to an extent. Because the manuscript is very heavily grounded in Catholic concepts, I wanted to make sure to keep widely accessible entry points for less religious readers, and using a well-known angel was one way to do that.

4. The series of poems that begin "The Angel Gabriel Texts Me..." stand out both structurally and in the way religious language is interpreted through worldly elements. Tell us about your process in creating these connections.

My intention with these pieces was to show the process of someone who has an entirely theoretical understanding of the world--and religious concepts, as a result--experiencing the practical application of those concepts. I was very deliberate about each religious term I chose for each piece, and I went on to choose strong images that I believed embodied those terms. However, I also wanted to communicate something slightly different in each of the three pieces. In the first piece, The Angel Gabriel is encountering the world for the first time and is really struggling with how to reconcile these pure, religious concepts with the realities of the world. In the second piece, I wanted to show the growing disillusionment The Angel Gabriel feels over the course of the narrative. In the final piece, I was more focused on showing how the religious concepts could be applied to The Angel Gabriel looking back on the end of his relationship with the speaker and applying those concepts to their time together.

5. One of the pivotal poems is "The Angel Gabriel Cheats at Scrabble." It feels as though this is a moment when the atheist narrator is metaphorically wrestling with the nature of religion. What values do you see represented here and how do they clash?

In my mind, the core value at the center of this piece is one of respect. Namely, what is acceptable in our treatment of others, and how should we treat those with whom we are closest? In my mind, the "magic" taking place during this board game is almost second in importance to the choices made by The Angel Gabriel when he decides that cheating and being a sore winner are more important than preserving a respectful relationship with the speaker. The larger questions in the piece can also be applied to the broader theological question. At its core, many religious and philosophical questions can be boiled down to this one: how should we treat others? I see this piece as The Angel Gabriel and the speaker discovering that they answer that question very differently, ultimately leading to a rift in the relationship.

Acknowledgements

I would like to thank the editors of the journals where some of these pieces first appeared or are forthcoming:

Atticus Review: "The Angel Gabriel Goes Black Friday Shopping" and "The Angel Gabriel Tries to Ghost Me"

Cutbow Quarterly: "The Angel Gabriel Texts Me Pictures from His First Week on Earth"

HAD: "The Angel Gabriel is on a Mission"

JAKE: "The Angel Gabriel Appears to Me," "The Angel Gabriel Brought Me a Message," and "The Angel Gabriel Goes to Open Mic Night"

Peatsmoke: "The Angel Gabriel Talks Me Off the Ledge" (as "The Angel Gabriel Talks Me Out of It") and "The Angel Gabriel Says It's Not a Booty Call if He Doesn't Have Genitals"

Acknowledgements

Thanks, of course, to Karen Cline-Tardiff for believing in this manuscript, and for reading it with such care. Thanks as well to my editor, Tiffany Woodley, for the attentive reading and feedback. Wendy, Matthew, and Ben: your generous readings of my work means more to me than I can say. To my writing group, especially: Robert, Bethany, Alex, Stefanie, Tim, Molly, Rorisang, and Will, thank you for the feedback that guided many of these pieces. And of course, to Kris, the first and final reader of every word of this manuscript: no thanks can ever truly be enough.

Author Bio

Frances Klein (she/her) is an Alaskan poet and teacher writing at the intersection of disability and gender. She is the 2022 winner of the Robert Golden Poetry Prize, and the author of the chapbooks New and Permanent (Blanket Sea 2022) and The Best Secret (Bottlecap Press 2022).